The HOUSE of who you are

poems & prayers to support your journey home

Kathleen Pizzello

Dedicated to
the Sun, the Moon
& the Stars

Table of Contents

The House of Who You Are

build yourself a throne
in the house of who you are

make yourself a crown
of the most beautiful flowers
from your soul
be the hero of your own life
be who you were born to be
you are every character of your own epic journey
you are the one you've been waiting for
heal yourself
so that you can show up in this world
as a beacon of light
to guide others
to build their own throne
to craft their own crown
and to realize
that they too are strong enough
to spread this healing light

this is the love that will change the world

Holy Water

Your tears
are holy water
from the wellspring
of your soul

Arcoiris

I am born of the dark
rooted to the Earth
through a strand of ruby red stones
expanding wombward
swirling saffron
sweet orange
rising sun fire
amber embers
breath of heart
emerald greens of unconditional love
chanting waves of turquoise
singing my song
indigo of intuition
ancient internal intelligence
Guide me to the sky!
amethyst lotus petals
bursting and blossoming
inviting angelic illumination
creating a rainbow bridge
from earth to sky

The Way Home

It was not on any map

The path of the heart
is written in the cosmos
Its lanterns are lit by stars
Its roads paved of experience

Somehow
I always knew
that the way was *through*
Angels & Ancestors walking with me
on all sides
Earth below me
Sky above me

Who needs a map?

The wind
she tells me where to go
and I say
Yes

I walk the path
of the courageous heart
I follow constellations
as my map
And the times
that I have loved
And the times
that I have lost
I move with
the breath of the mountains
the currents of the sea
and the light of the moon

I am the map
I am the path
I am the journey

I am the destination

I am home

Boundless

let your heart
keep breaking open
it will become
b o u n d l e s s
and so
will
you

A Lover

What are the ways
in which you live
for love itself?
It used to be that
I longed for a lover
to meet me
in the house of who I am
But now
I pray
every day
to meet myself
as my own beloved
to grow my own flowers
to write my own love letters
to tell myself that
I am beautiful
that I am worthy of love
But still
there is this alive hope
deep down
that someday
I will walk
into a field
praised by the sun
loved by the moon
it's land layered in wild flowers
and I will meet you there

This Vessel

What a gift
to be awake
and alive
in this body

Grateful
for this vessel
and its ability
and willingness
to move
in strange
and familiar ways

It's almost like
it knows
but doesn't
at the same time
the soul
exploring the house
it has been given
for this lifetime
surprised by the alchemy
that is born from the flow
of freedom
of breath
of blood
and bones
and stardust

Forgiveness

One thing I need
that I demand
in relationship
is to forgive
and be forgiven

We are all
just tumbling
through
time
and space

We are floating in space

Let's forgive each other

Patient Dreams

Let go of the tight grip
that you have on your dreams
treat your dreams
like your lover
bathe them in your attention
but let there be a flow
of equal energy
between you
an equilibrium of respect
and patience
for the dream to blossom
in its own time
and in its own way

Heart Seams

if my heart had seams
they'd be made of
golden threads
lovingly
holding
together
the memoirs of
every emotion
I've ever felt
every failure
I've endured
every love loved
every cry of laughter
and tears too

if you journey
into my heart
there is a reservoir
of sacred tears
holy water
from the wellspring of my soul
it is here that I go
to remember the depths
of who I am
who I have been
and who I am becoming
and I know now
that what holds my heart together
is made of gold
because of the alchemy
that is born
from returning to yourself

going home
again and again
to the house
of who you are
to the altar
of your heart

Mother Ocean

Mother Ocean
called me home
I needed respite
from the desert
which was blazing

and it was she
who held the capacity
of me

She drew me in
to her watery womb
and held me
in her immense
embrace

I surrendered
as she washed away
the pain of days
and the dust of disorder

I rode a wave
to the shore
of emergence
a holy genesis
born from
and supported by
her

She reminded me
again
of a different way
of being

allowing the flow
of mother ocean's
sacred tears
to stream
and navigate
the terrain
of my body

I layed down
to the Earth
heart to heart
feeling Her rhythm
and vibration
and filling my own vessel
with all of that magic

I grabbed a bunch
of my salty sea hair
and breathed Her—
she who holds
the capacity
of me—
then I stuck out
my tongue
and tasted her
briny delight
on my sunkissed
summer lips
and I smiled

In the Desert

In the desert
you'll be told
different things
like to strip down
naked
to your soul
and let go of
your bullshit

She will invite you to rise
just before dawn
so that you can see
the star spangled sky
as she fades
and passes the torch
to the mighty sun

I read once
that the desert
will show you
all that you need to see
she is fierce in her ways
her intensity intimidating
but she invited you
because you are ready
to dance with the sun

Empowerment

Empower your movements
with the feeling
of your intentions

Grace

Grace your day
with the beauty
of your intentions

Sacred Rebirth

I want to come undone
to fully unravel myself
freely & wholly
nude to the world
no reservations
because I don't care
what you think anymore
what I care about
is how broken my heart is
and yours too
and I know yours is broken too
because just being alive
in this world
will do that to you

but also
I wanted to tell you
it's ok to be broken
let everything
fall a p a r t
become ruins
and dust
become nothing
return to the void
that you were born from
the wellspring
that lives deep
deep down
inside the house of who you are
go there
again and again
drink from this well

and use its wisdom
to nurture a new dream of being
plant your seed
in your own dust
where you once died
and returned home
be patient
allow there to be
a current of love
waves of grace
and respect
for your dream
and your own
sacred rebirth

Weaving Destiny

Destiny has a way
of weaving its golden thread
around certain souls
who are blessed
to come together
in sacred and brave space
with permission to be
exactly who they are

Let's allow ourselves
to be so vulnerable
dear ones
that our truths
whatever they are
guide us over bridges
from fear to freedom

We can walk together

Resilience

The moment I fell to my knees
in full surrender
my pain took my hand
and lovingly said
I wanted to show you
How strong you are
How resilient you are
How brave you are
and when I cleared the tears from my eyes
I looked up and realized
my pain was my power

Relationship

the longest
most intimate
most painful
most loving
most revealing
relationship
is the one
I have
with myself
it is multifaceted
complicated
complex
and filled with surprises
a holy trinity
of
body
mind
spirit
each part
an education
a teaching
an unveiling
of the wisdom
that each
has to offer
to the integrity
of my being

Praises

Praises to the Earth
the direction of the North
May we remember where we walk
and what is below us

Praises to the Fire
the direction of the South
May we transmute and transform
what is within us

Praises to the Water
the direction of the West
May we flow with the tides of our lives
and be brave enough to feel deeply

Praises to the Air
the direction of the East
May we be infinitely inspired
by all that surrounds us

To all Above
To all Below
To all Within
and all Without
To the entire Universe
and to your very Soul

May we walk in peace
May we breathe clean air
May we recognize each other
For who we truly are
May we let go of all that wounds

and embrace that which supports
each individual to share their gifts
in vulnerability and truth
May we celebrate the beauty
of the Earth
the Sky
our breath
life itself
the desire to be
to live and to truly love
ourselves and each other

May it be so
It is so
And so it is

Blessed Be

Love River

If my love was a river
it would be sourced
from the highest peak
on the mountain of my heart
it would run through my being
winding and wandering
longing to flow and find its way
into the ocean of you

Revolution of the Soul

I wonder if
it pains a flower
to blossom open
the way it hurts
to play the edge
of my own human capacity

both lead to
an expansive opening
an unfurling
of the outer layers
exposing the hidden jewels
the nectar that dwells
in the deepest places
of who we are

this is the alchemy
the great mystery
the weaving
of pain and pleasure
shadow and light
left and right

When we allow
the sacred dance
of the self
holding nothing back
fully surrendered
to the truth of what is
what was
and all that could possibly be
there is an honoring

a reverence
for life itself
it's the process
the journey
there's no rushing
only allowing
being present
showing up
the best way we can
each day
each moment
each precious breath

One day we notice
through everything
the blossom begins to open
each petal of experience
yearning to be noticed
to be seen
and then eventually
ready to be released
to the Earth

What is given is forgiven
we allow all of us to be seen
as we are
naked
bare
unveiled
no part unworthy
of the sun

Finally
each petal falls
revealing what's left
of its earthly vessel
perhaps a stem
some seeds
or bones

they can be given too
back to the ground
invited to rest
to return
to dissolve
to become one

A full revolution
of the soul

Rainstorm

When I feel sad
I invite a rainstorm
to pour out of me
letting the sky burst open
through my heart
releasing the storm
letting it unfold
and reveal itself
as thunder
lightning
rain

In time its rhythm slows
the calm after the storm
it smells like the Earth
wet with my emotions
and I am free
I a m   f r e e
for now anyway
and that is good enough
the sky affirms
by painting itself
with an arc of color
reminding me
of the beauty
that is born
in the letting go

An Offering

There is a flower
at the root of my heart
it pulsates
opening and closing

All that is holy within me
All that is broken
All that is alive
All that has yet to be born

I offer everything
I offer everything
To the fire of transformation

Epic View

The only destination
that is worthy of your being
is the house of who you are

Once you find your way there
build yourself a throne
take a high seat

and make sure
the view is epic

Equinox

The great wheel
takes another turn
as we walk the threshold
of seasons and cycles

the great Mother is preparing to rest
she is a crone once again
her skin weathered
with experience
and tired from long days
in the sun

Praise the sun
for the light it has gifted us
and the power
and potential
that was born
in its glory

Eat your fruits now
and enjoy it, won't you?
for what you've created
is asking to be enjoyed

Now light and dark
dance together
but only for a breath
and then we honor
the great exhale
the sunset of the season
the dark days
of turning inward
the veils grow thin
the wisdom deepens
we let things go
releasing
releasing
exhaling

How I Pray

How do you pray?

This is what I do:
I touch the Earth
I feel the wind on my skin
I let my spirit move me
I laugh
I find pleasure
I pour tears
and let my heart break
I make love
to life itself

I wake up every day
in awe
of existence

This is how I pray

Your Body Is a Temple

your body is a temple

your bones
house the stories
of your ancestors

your blood
carries the secrets
of the ancients

your cells
contain the mysteries
of the universe

your heart
holds the wisdom
of the worlds

Rooted in Love

Whatever you do
Whatever you stand for
Let it be rooted in love

Shadow + Light

this is me
living
in
love
for
life
itself
all its pains + it's pleasures
d a n c i n g
finding my own way
shadow + light

Waves

how do you ride
the tides
of your existence?

Witches

blessed are we
who believe in
the power
our own m a g i c

May You Be Free

May you be
free to wander
every day
of your life

Beltane

praise the Earth
glorious sun!
feminine + masculine
divinely dance
plant the seeds
of your heart blossom
shine the beauty
of your soul
finding rhythm
in the pulsation
of life

I Love You

blessed be this beautiful earth

blessed be your beautiful body

blessed be your beautiful heart

I love you

Blessed Be the Light

blessed be the light
that illuminates the path
that we are being asked to walk

blessed be the darkness
that is asking to be seen
heard
and acknowledged
so that we can let die
what needs to die
and create a tender space
for a new way
to be born
the tomb
becomes the womb
the dark place
of endings
and beginnings

blessed be the light
that returns
to meet the darkness
tending the seeds
of our desires
and giving us hope
for new beginnings

blessed be the sun
the moon
the stars
the earth
the air
the fire
the waters
the heavens
all that is above
all that is below
all that is within
and all that is without

Wild Spirit

blessed be the wild spirit
that lives in this body

you are worthy of love
you are worthy of joy

you can use your pain
as an instrument
to sing the song
of who you are

when you allow yourself to be seen
in raw vulnerability
as you truly are

you invite others
to do the same
to be seen
and heard

we invite each other
to heal together
turning pain
into power
poison into nectar
enemy into friend

we are the alchemists
of our own experience
and I believe
with my the entirety
of my wild heart
this
is the love
that will change
the world

Yes

trust
patience
devotion

the willingness to be
exactly who you are
in this very moment
is a brave way
of living

I say Y E S

You Are Beautiful

be who you are

it is so *b e a u t i f u l*

In This Moment

so much complexity
to this existence
so many waves

and in this moment

I am h a p p y

Heart Cave

that which wishes
to be revealed
is sometimes buried
deep within the cave
of the heart

life can make it
hard to remember
and easy to forget
that it is life itself
who is teaching us
how to open the heart
time and time again
and discover that
it is in the willingness
to stay open
where the treasure resides
it is the alchemy of the heart
the dance of the soul
shadow + light
pleasure + pain
the journey of the spirit
riding epic waves
of poison + nectar
highs + lows

but choosing
to see the beauty
to be the beauty
that surrounds us

and saying yes
to love
again
and
again

I say Y E S

Fearless Heart

the fearless heart
is not without fear
the fearless heart
says *hello*
to the fear
dances with it
gets to know it
not denying
but acknowledging
not avoiding
but embracing
choosing authenticity
over expectation
living with integrity

Thank You

Thank you disappointment for making me vulnerable
Thank you rage for lighting a fire inside of me
Please help me transmute that energy
into something positive and productive for the world
Thank you sadness for making me feel so deeply
Thank you to those who lack integrity for showing me who I
    don't want to be
Thank you to those who live with integrity for inspiring me to
    live in that way

Thank you life
Thank you for your intensity
magic
surprises
highs
lows
and all in betweens
I offer all that I am
I am grateful
I bow in reverence
to all that was
to all that is
and to all the infinite possibilities of what will be

Angels & Allies

when you are walking
through fire
call upon
your lions
your tigers
angels
and ancestors
the priestesses
and fae folk
pachamama
the starseeds
and anyone else
who has your back
your front
your left + right
above you
and below you

The Key

thank you universe
for the gift
of my life

for breaking my heart
wide open
so that I can truly feel
all that I am

thank you fear
for making me brave

thank you passion
for driving me
to do what I love

thank you teachers
for guiding me to the threshold
of my heart
helping me find the key
and the encouragement
to open the door

Blessings

may you release what no longer resonates with your soul
may you appreciate what the world is teaching you
may you create space for something beautiful in your life
may you walk your path with ease
when you don't find ease may you find friends to laugh and
    cry with
may you be seen and heard
may you love and be loved
may you use your body in ways that feel free
give you strength
and liberate your heart
may you know the beauty of your story
your life
and who you are

Lifelong Goal

lifelong goal:

cultivate a fearless heart
and expand into my courage
to be who I truly am

Gift of Life

thank you
great sun
for the gift
of life
and the opportunity
to be who I am

An Invitation

I invite you
and I invoke you
to create a ritual practice
where you can discover
and be
who you truly are

Power of Love

it is my fundamental belief
that the power of love
is more vital
than the love of power

this is the love
that will change
the world

Let Life Blow Your Mind

let life blow your mind
just by living it

Life Is Beautiful

life is beautiful
even when it hurts

When You Listen

when you listen to
and follow
the deepest whispers
of your heart
your life will change
it is not always easier
but it is more beautiful

Call It In

call in
the highest expression
of who you are

Gracious

when the universe
provides everything
you need
accept
with a gracious heart

For Real

let's just be
who we really are

The Real Ones

spend more time
with people who
support your evolution
and love you
for who you are
becoming

To Be Seen

to be seen and held
by another human

to be told
you are beautiful

to be told
you shine

this is the love
that will change
the world

Myrrh Maiden

myrrh maiden:

a mystical siren
who swims
with the tides of life
and rides waves of love
into the sunset
to the moon
and back again

Rinse & Repeat

forgive
(yourself + others)
release
love
let go
feel
and do it over
and over
again
and again
until you find
p e a c e

Heart Breath

let your heart b r e a t h e

The Sweetest Thing

how to keep
your heart young:

listen to children
use your imagination
play with dogs
walk barefoot
create art
love without expectation
be exactly who you are

but most importantly
eat icecream
with real cream + sugar
and no napkins
let the ice cream
paint your lips
and cheeks
the tip of your nose
then let your dog
or your lover
lick it off

the sweetest thing

Let Your Love Fly

Can you fully give yourself
to the fire that burns around you
and within you?

Surrender to the forces
of transformation

Give your pain
Your joy
Your ritual
Your breath

Give everything

Let it be taken
It's not yours anyway
Let it go

Then be empty
Be open
Be free

Let life flow through you
Let love flow through you
It's not to be held onto
Its like gripping the air
Or holding a wave
In the palm
of your hand

It is all temporary
Fleeting

It flies
It flies
Like a bird
To us
And then away again

So love
Love as much as you possibly can
In each moment
Each life you are given
But let it be free
Let it go
Love and let it go
Let your love be free
A flow of freedom
Let it fly
Let it fly
Like a bird

Let your love fly

Sensitivity Is A Super Power

honor your sensitivity

Depression

I woke up depressed
with the weight of the worlds
on my chest

There was no escaping it

so I took a bath
in my sadness

I let it wash all over me

I ate my pain for breakfast
I took a walk with my darkness
I planted some roses with my loneliness

The feelings
apparently were enjoying
my company

so they stayed for cocktails
and dinner too
I could tell
they wanted to make love
so I took them to bed with me

Live With Intention

Inspired by and written for Mary Anne Radmacher

each day
when you rise
salute the sun
and give thanks
for the gift of your life

take time
to sit
be with your breath
and remember
the miracle
that it is
to be alive

say a prayer
for yourself
those you love
and those who challenge you
send your love
in every direction
gracing the north
the south
the east and west
above and below
within and without
with the essence of
your holy heart

move your body
make it a ritual
the prayer embodied
let it come alive
let it fill your vessel
the house of who you are
and then offer it all
offer it to the earth
to the sky
to the air
and to the waters
and to those who came before

as you move through
the rhythm of your day
show up courageously
be who you are
speak your truth
practice patience
and kindness
lead with your heart
take time to listen
and be with others
spend time with yourself
and be with nature

when the day is done
and the sun begins to fade
beyond the horizon
take a moment of silence
and stillness
to recognize the beauty
that exists all around you
draw a gentle awareness
back to your breath
give thanks
for this day
for all that you have witnessed
and for all the possibilities
of tomorrow

look up at the starlit sky
praise the moon
feel your smallness
and your greatness
dancing together
infinitely
through time + space

Things To Do Slowly

things to do slowly
1. walk
2. make love
3. eat
4. hug
5. start your day
6. drink tequila

Nature

Nature reminds us
of the mastery of god

Let Love

let love
    transform you

Vastness

how is it that
my heart
once felt
like a turbulent sea
and now
it has taken
refuge
in the desert
where it feels

v a s t
b a r r e n
o p e n

and no longer
broken

Burn It Down

we must find
hope
in tending to
that which
needs repair

and if it is
beyond repair

burn
that
shit
down

Loving Yourself

loving yourself
is your destiny

Infinity

infinity is flowing
at the center
of your heart
the energy of the earth
unites with the cosmos
above and below
become one
inner marriage
of elements
archetypes
and
energies
flow
dance
ecstatic
making love
creating
sustaining
dissolving
into
the
eternity
of
existence

This Mountain

this mountain we've been climbing
feels insurmountable
immeasurable
and never ending

great mountain
please teach me
to be brave
to stay humble
to not give up

I want to see the view
to breathe that air
I can feel it

each step feels like
we are on a million mile march
an uphill battle
with the world
and each other

if I needed water
would you help me
quench my thirst?

will you help me tend my wounds
from this expedition?
there are so many

it's not just me
we are all begging
to be held
by each other

there is so much space
at the top
for all of us
it's clear up there
vast sky
freedom
the heart bursts
upon arrival
limitless

I'll meet you there

Cosmic Embrace

the sky
is calling out to us
sending us waves
of love
telling us
be brave,
you are in
a constant
flow
of
cosmic embrace

Brave In The Darkness

Lead me out
of the wreckage
of my mind

Remind me
of my brilliance
that is ever present
beyond the ignorance

Help me
mine diamonds
from the bitterness
of my past

Let me realize
and recognize
the mystery
of this fragile existence

give me strength
to forgive
every injustice
I've encountered
especially towards myself

Help me be brave
in the darkness

Help me be brave
in the darkness

Help me be brave
in the darkness

Guide me
from my deepest fears
to my most radical
unbound freedom
to be who I am

Make me a vessel
of beauty and truth

May it be so

It is so

Radiant Emergence

the snake is ready
to begin its
uncoiling ascent
rising from an
ancient sleep
through my body
offering new life
awakening my bones
reminding me
of the power
within me and
giving birth to a
radiant e m e r g e n c e

For Bubba

sometimes
we are blessed
and the Universe
sends us a sweet fur friend
they come to teach us
how to love beyond what we know
they teach us to serve
to walk with another
and eventually they teach us how to let go
how to say goodbye
with grace
what evolved souls
to teach us the most important lessons
in our lives
to love and to let go
to love and let go
to know we will have to say goodbye
but still love with everything we have
this is true grace
this is grace

Whispers

your sensitivity is sacred
within it lies
ancient understanding
millions of years
of evolution
your ancestors
learned for you
wisdom passed
through your bones
as a gift
from beyond
the beyond

listen to your bones
the whispers
of where you came from
and the truth
of experience

Choices

Life is a journey
of constant choice
the choice to stay the same
or the choice to become something greater
stasis or a process of discovery, growth, adventure

do the world a favor
choose your own evolution
be the revolution
that everyone needs

be the one who rises up
who sets the example
do not retreat
gather the lions
walk onward
keep looking inward
consult your heart
for wisdom and deep feeling
call on your guides
know you are never alone
you play an important role
in this collective experience

be kind
ask for help
rest often
forgive yourself
be of service
practice ritual that you make up
pray for the world
go outside

forgive your family
keep dreaming
heal your wounds
don't question your worthiness
keep your boundaries
but keep your heart open
make eye contact
listen
consume citrus
create
you are here to create
for the sake of creating
doing
being
expressing
your beautiful soul
don't hold back
not one bit
shine your light
be brave
be you
show up in the world
exactly as you are
that is your gift
it is a choice
to share it

Circles

path of life
circle of spirit
wheel of karma
no end and no beginning
swimming in two different directions
going nowhere and everywhere
at once
time dissolves
life becomes death
death becomes life
being born again and again
through the tail of the dragon
returning
through the mouth of destiny
returning returning
because where everything ends
everything begins
the illusion of life
is that everything is separate
but the truth is intertwined
within all of us
everything connected
an invisible force
of knowing
that must be rediscovered
mined for
and treasured

Castles

all the castles
of the kingdom
stood protected
by moats of stone
and beasts with
big teeth

they felt safe
with their guards up
borders and boundaries
protecting them
from what was on
the outside

I was on the outside
not able to hide
or hold in
all that I was
nothing could keep me
I was wild, they said
but to me
it was about being free
about being real

even when I tried
to be part of the kingdom
it couldn't hold me
so it spat me out

I had to learn
how to survive
on the outside

where you are exposed
to all sorts of weather
of experience
quakes and storms
sunrises
and sunsets
set the rhythm
the earth held me
and the elements
became allies
the wind showed me
where to go
and the mountains
they taught me how to stay
how to just be
who I was
and nothing else

now, the desert is teaching me
resilience
the castles still stand
but have turned
to faded shapes
in the distance

I invite in a gentle peace
surrounded by my faithful companions
and at home with myself
a twinge of heartache
for those who
never leave
will never know
the wisdom
of being wild

Epic Adventure

I let go
and again
wind to sail
rudder to sea
swaying
like a snake

I'm still the captain of this ship
with no compass
but the pain
of my own experience
of this life
now the sea
is sand
desert high
spirit
stay true
keep sailing
sand and sea
just keep moving
through the tides
you'll meet your mates
along the way
let the moon
soothe the ache
of fallen expectations
and broken heartedness
keep the sails open
heart too
w i d e   o   p   e   n
to the winds
one day

you will catch
the tide
the wave
the wonder
the first mate
that will swiftly change
the course
of your destiny
and become
your most
epic adventure

The Weeping Walk

the path called so
I went for a weeping walk
and had a heart to heart
with the land

my loneliness
was embraced by the sun
and I smiled
as the path invited me in
and I felt again
that I belonged to something great
something beautiful
and I wept
in gratitude
as I climbed
the curves of her hills
the junipers telling me
that life can still bloom
in the shadow of
your winter
and that gave me strength
to keep going
and the wind
it was like the wind
was carrying me home
to myself
and clearing away
all of the pains
of this existence
and others too

I came upon a stone throne
and it offered itself to me
so a sat and wept some more
I sent a string of rubies
deep into the earth
so she knew I was here
and she did

I let the sun drench me
with its light medicine
I painted my tears
on my third eye
and my heart
as I watched the red tailed hawks
dancing for me
the freedom dance
the beauty way
allowing the unfolding
at peace with what is
moving
floating
flying
existing beyond
what is here
what we see
going deeper
into the mysteries
of what it is
to truly feel
and truly be
alive

Stillness

a moment
of silence
stillness
solitude
resting with the earth
reflecting inward
a humble offering
of self
to the fire of transformation
a slow, steady turning
of the ancient wheel
a stirring
the flame flickers
an awakening
a whisper
to unwind
to unbind
to become
to emerge
renewed and radiant
like the sun

Sun & Moon

light of the sun
I strengthen my vessel
light of the moon
I surrender to my sensitivity
under the sun
I am the lion
under the moon
I am the wolf
both roar
and howl
are spoken here

Hope

bless these great mountains
that we climb
protect us
as we transcend layers
of atmosphere
and self

we leave behind what
we no longer
choose to carry
the burdens
the lessons
the heartaches
we let it go
placing it to the ground
with gratitude
offering it all
to the earth

rising up
strength of body
wisdom of mind
brightness of spirit
gazing to the horizon
of the unknown
of possibly
and liberation

there is a newness
a hope of beginning
creating new ways
of living and being

and one day
we all make it
to the peak
we go higher
than the horizon
we go
beyond where
we could have
ever imagined

we look around
at each other
we respect
and honor
each
individual
journey

then as a collective
we tilt our heads
to the sky
and we say
We Are Free

Dance

dipping my toe
into unfamiliar waters

the human capacity
to feel
fear
excitement
dread
and delight
all in one breath
will never cease
to blow my mind

an invitation
to a foreign place
I've never been
yet unknowingly
yearning to discover
a new hand to hold
mysterious eyes to gaze
a fresh horizon
of adventure
discoveries
hidden treasures
a portal to worlds
that only need to be
created
to be known

so when the unfamiliar
extends its embrace
calling you
to come dance
this tango of exploration
I hope you dance

Touch The Earth

Touch the earth
remember where you are
reach to the sky
remember where you came from
touch your heart
remember who you are

As dawn breaks
a radiant emergence arises
streaking the light of god/goddess
across the ocean of sky
I am reminded of the miracle
and the mystery
that it is to be alive

I open my heart
and my senses
to the journey
that anticipates my arrival
I offer myself fully to this day
and I bow to
this opportunity
to truly live
and be who I am

Kiss The Earth

when I walk
upon this mighty land
I ask my feet
to kiss the earth
for my arms to embrace the wind
like a lover
then let it go
unfurling my heart wings
and leaning back
revealing myself freely to the temple of the sky
so the stars can see me
exactly as I am
dancing in appreciation
of this site of holy pilgrimage
there is nowhere to go
nowhere to be
other that right here
exactly where you are
bow down
touch the earth
and breathe with her
tell her your stories
your sorrows
your hopes and dreams
she listens
like a great mother
offer yourself
to this space
again
and again
until you feel your arrival
to the most holy

the most sacred
the highest altar
of who you are
the gateway
to the heaven
of you

Today I Choose

Today I choose
I choose to rise in awareness
of the world around me
and the world within me
I choose to delight
in the inhabitance
of this being
and this body

I tend to the experience
of my soul
and listen
I listen to the yearnings
of the ancient grail
that dwells inside of me

This is what it says:
You are holy
You are worthy
You are not this or that
You are everything
Everything that you see
is a reflection of yourself
You are the pain
You are the rain
You are the flower
You are the brilliance
of one thousand suns

Shine your light
and turn towards the darkness
For it is in the dance
of the two
that we drink the
soma from the cup
of wisdom

Finding God

If you want to find God
look for the beauty
that exists and lives
in all beings

Open the eyes of your heart
and then
watch the sun rise
and set

Spend time
with innocents
and wisdom keepers
let them teach you
and remind you
of the radiance
that exists
around you
and within you

Then look at yourself
look deeply
into your own eyes
into your own heart
and know
that all of the beauty
that you see
is a reflection
of your own
divine Self

Alchemical Journey

I am woven
of golden threads
made from
love
laughter
sorrow
anger
courage
fear
despair
wonder
peace
and more

all are welcome
and embraced
in the house
of who I am
weaving
a great tapestry
creating
sustaining
dissolving
concealing
revealing
rising
in an infinite dance
of fire and nectar
shadow and light

a sammelana
of co creation
and transformation
with the Universe
that lives within me
and without me
above me
and below me

the alchemical journey
of the soul

Howl

remember to howl

About the Writer

"She who is sovereign to herself" Kathleen Pizzello, a Virgo Sun, has been on the long and winding path of the journey of the self since she can remember. Always wanting to dive deep, uncover, and discover. She is a mystic, a poetess, a deep feeler, a wild woman, and a priestess of the moon. She follows the way of the wind, and because of that has been blessed to live and travel many places on this beautiful earth, and that inspires her life and writing.

In the 3rd grade, Kathleen's poem "A Plain Spring Day" received an award in the seaside New England town where she grew up. Although she found joy in writing and it ran through her like a river, her writing remained mostly academic and work related until she moved to the high desert of California during the pandemic in 2020.

One day it came to her attention that one of her favorite poets, Mary Anne Radmacher, was leading a poetry group online. Led by instinct and a hint of childlike excitement, she joined the group. Guided by prompts and lots of love, the group blossomed together, and Kathleen rediscovered her voice-and a special sort of grace- through poetry. It was therapeutic and so needed at that very moment. It was there that Kathleen decided that she wanted to pursue her longtime-somewhat-hidden dream of becoming a published poet. She is so grateful for every being, experience, and teaching that has inspired her and brought her to this moment.

She has been a teacher for over ten years, has countless hours of diverse training, and founded her business **the moon + the mat** in 2017. Kathleen's offerings come from a deep place of love, service, and authenticity. Her experience includes thousands of hours of yoga teacher training, 5 years of teaching middle school social studies, traveling the world, bodywork, energy healing, ritual magic, astrology and the path of the priestess. She is in deep dedication to the rhythms of the moon, the earth, and the rising of consciousness on the planet. She shares joyfully, offering healing alignment, depth yet lightheartedness, and cultivation of a fearless heart. Her intention is to guide readers to a place of freedom in their bodies, minds, and hearts. The invitation is to be who you are. It is with immense gratitude that she writes and shares her heart. Kathleen currently resides in the high desert of California with her beloved animal allies and continues to offer classes and other services via the moon + the mat online studio. She also guides retreats worldwide and teaches locally in Joshua Tree, California.

Thank you for reading these words from my heart!

I'd love to stay connected.
You can find me here:

www.themoonandthemat.com
themoonandthemat@gmail.com
@kathleen_pizzello
@themoonandthemat

Please share my work and tag – I'd so appreciate it!

Loving you to the moon and beyond ... beyond the beyond!

With Immense Gratitude,
Kathleen